Stories
He Told

ORIGINAL POEMS BY
Bart Laemmel

Copyright © 2016 by Bart Laemmel
bart@b2buildingscience.com

All rights reserved. Published 2016
Printed in the United States of America
19 18 17 16   1 2 3 4

ISBN 978-0-692-81016-3
Library of Congress Cataloging-in-Publication Data available upon request

No part of this book may be used or reproduced in any manner whatsoever without written permission, except in the case of brief quotations embodied in critical articles or reviews.

Cover illustration by Bart Laemmel
Cover and book design, editing, layout and production by Marjorie DeLuca

Published by
AGS Publishing
948 Vitos Way · Carbondale, CO 81623
info@aspengfx.com

Stories He Told

Summer Maine

I see you summer Maine
A dirt path winding from the road
Here is first growth forest
Poplar, birch and blueberry race
To claim the meadow space,
While thornberry and alder vie for
Sunlight on the lane. And spruce,
Mighty spruce—even now in the pasture.
Destined to be lord of the wood
At some distant time.

I see a parade of granite
Sometimes Saco white and sometimes
Showy red as by Bar Harbor's shore.
As an old Indian woman grinding corn
The ancient ice smoothed and pressed it down to
Where now river fingers meet the tide.
Giant blocks keep rooflines straight
Against a thousand storms and
Islets and a hundred harbors make
From which men launch against the sea
It undergirds and is the foundation
Strength from which its citizens claim, Dirigo!

I see an eagle on its winged course,
An inspection of its littoral realm.
It soars o'er green meadows hard pressed
By the forest side, the great trees felled away
But only enough it seems to let humankind
Claim their space. But more, the eagle, the loops
And circles of its flight a longhand signature in
The sky that man and nature can be one.
I see you summer Maine,
Nor can my mind's eye forget.

—WILLIAM LAEMMEL

CONTENTS

Summer Maine	v
NATURE	**1**
Crispness	3
It's My Island	4
Small	5
Morning Mist 1	6
Morning Mist 2	6
The Giant	7
Autumn	8
My Season	9
Thrown About	10
OBSERVATION	**11**
Undone	13
Her Fever	14
Built	15
Hello?	16
Hillsides	17
Long Distance	18
Short 1	19
Short 2	19
Short 3	19
Short 4	19
Short 5	19
Down	20
Pulling of Three	21
I Don't See It That Way	22
New and Improved	23
Middle	24
Sunflowers	25
Forgetting	26
I Forgot	27
Throw Them Back	28
The King	29

CONTENTS

Unleashed	30
Sure to Last	31
Weight	32
Back Again	33

INSIDE — **35**

Checking In	37
Chasing	38
Hiding Things	40
Judgement	41
Hero	42
Communication	43
Motivation	44
Sleep Walking	45
In My Head	46
Infinity	47
Eastern Rain	48
What I See	50
Thin	51
Influence	52
Everything	53
Head-Long	54

LYRICAL — **55**

Broken Love Songs	57
Fly On	58
Stunning	59
Otherwise	60
When I Cry	61
Cruelty	62
Spinning	63
Baby Come	64

HEART — **65**

Moving On	67
Brilliance	68
Burn	69

Sheep	70
'Til Next Time	71
Daughter	72
Trust	73
Bring Us In	74

OTHERS   **75**

Sleep Deep	77
Heads up	78
Should I Think?	79
Starry Nights	80
Tranquil Waters	82
Details	83
Deep of You	84
Care	85
I'm the Fool	86
Stay In Me	87
Gone the Day	88
Love of Dogs	89
On Me	90
For You	91
All Lit-up	92
1% to All	93
Too Quick	94
Slip Away	95
Every Day	96
Morning After	97
Underneath It All	98
Black Water	99
Four Winds	100
Blurry	101

DEDICATION   **103**

Stories You Told	105

Nature

Crispness

White and blue and thin of air
This is the crispness I love
Trudging slow and thinking hard
The warmth of the winter sun
Springing me forward to change
In this jagged expanse
The snow is loosening its grip
On the evergreen
Slowly revealing treasures at every crest
This summit comes in pieces
Reminding me to lift my head
Halt my thoughts
Give myself a chance to witness
Give me a chance to find that space
Up here I could stay too long
Listen to the silence
Unpack my worries
Lose my colors to the white

It's My Island

Has the sun come up on your island?
Or has the wind blown the sea across the sky?
Once you wrote about the hot air balloons
But the time has come to sound the alarm

Nothing will take away the memory of youth
With the lovers lined up at your door
Don't choose for choosing's sake
The tide will come with the full moon

A groom will make himself ready
To save you from the rising storm
And deliver you from the indecision
That ties you down

Small

More black than brilliant
The night sky is dim and distant
To see how small we are
We must tend to our lights

Morning Mist 1

Crawling about the mountainside
In slow, steadying transformation
The pale morning mist
Is sliding and searching
Pulling the needles
From the stand
Pushing the gold
Into the early snow

Morning Mist 2

A slow moving line of mist
floated by my window this morning
Lighting up with early pink
Turning from the sun
Lifting up through the valley
And melting into the sky

The Giant

Bury me close to the sun
A high and scenic place
From where I can oversee
All that I have been
All that I have grown
Knowing that in my time and place
I confronted the fear and the unknown
That renders men blind to the horizon
And riddles them into paralysis

Autumn

Through the fluttering
    Yellow
        Chatter
Expands the cold, steady silence
    Bright
        Black
Drowning in apologies
    Drifting
        Sinking
The run down lifted him
    Rolling
        Blowing

My Season

Bare branches lay like lace upon the sunrise
Smoke from chimneys mock the early colors
The East is giving birth this morning
To the solstice and breaking us from our fall
I'm always amazed by these months
In this land named after Indians
And fought over by the French
Void of leaf and flower
This stark landscape hides no imperfections
Laying out before me like an old woman's body
Speaking the gospel of nature's voice
Down below, they crowd my sidewalk
With lingering breath
The bustle of the season is in full swing
Here I will sit enjoying this nervous view
Coffee brewing
I lay my eyes upon this crispness

Thrown About

Searched for on the low
Found on the ground
Broken off rough
Or tumbled smooth and round

Something in the shape
Palmed a perfect fit
Unsoiled and unbothered
On ancient shores they sit

Sent on its mission
Hurled upon the air
Caught in its sights
Inanimate objects beware

Skipped in competition
Only the flattest will do
10 times…14 times…!
Sometimes only two

Sitting on a shelf
A reminder of memories past
Taking me back to that day
How the years spin fast

Observation

Undone

Trouble settled across HER face
Unrest, discontent
Undone
So much for HER to do
Too much for HER to accomplish
All to be done by HER
For HER on HER watch
This is not about HIM
Not about the LOVE
Not about the NOW
Or the BEFORE
Or the ever-AFTER
HER cause is HER
HER is the UNDONE

Her Fever

Hold me to the fire
The cold, burning fire
Wet with judgement
And adorned in lace

Curiosity will catch her
Down in the tall grass
Far up on the hill
Chasing away her fever

Raise me up
Don't let me fall

Built

It's to the beauty that we tend
Keeping it alive
Against the dying light of time
Function is but a lucky convenience
Comfort is only known in its absences
The eye is keen
To what is pleasant
The mind does not want to look
Upon years of dusty neglect
Nothing is meaner than an object
Built in haste and disregard
So we tend to the beauty
Wheedling details into true proportion
Inspired dirt and stone
Leaf, bush and grass
This place is not then just space
But warmth wrapped around possibility
It is in the beauty we endure to strive

Hello?

Ok, your vacation is over
The coffee break is done
Time to go to work!
Time to maybe intervene

This land, this life,
Is not for us
For all our usefulness
Our progress, elusiveness
We have proven one thing
We are not bulletproof

Umm…are you listening?
Believe me, I can understand
Your frustration or disappointment
But trust me this
You will miss us
When we are gone

So bend us from our divine darkness
Bring us to the center
Before we break your heart anymore

Hillsides

Johnson stood on the hillside
The summer was full to him
The lupine had finally bloomed
Purple spires standing up to the sun
Making the hillside overwhelm the sky
He breathed in them all
And held on for just a little more
Soon this will vanish to gold
To brown, to white, to mud
Up against the year, these colors are fleeting
Johnson stood to the warm breeze
Closing his eyes to the sun in the west
As it is today, tomorrow and beyond
The sun will always fade to dusk
He stood to say goodbye
To understand just a little more
And to give greeting to the chill left behind
The calm was thick in his eyes
The night was far beyond night
Slowly growing, expanding outside
What he could conceive
Johnson felt his smallness
He could sneak around the edges of the air
Hide in the soft rustle of the leaves
Here there was nothing
Just plain old nothing
Here he could imagine
Yet imagine being nothing more

Long Distance

If I sailed 100 miles for love,
Would love wait on the hilltop?
(Watching) for the dreary sails to breach,
Bold on the dry, bloody horizon

But if I never (love), I'll never hurt
or be looked over, (left behind),
or taken along
My insecurities lead me
Forward to conformity
With my indifference, to death,
to colors unearthed by bliss

Bend to the crosses (burning)
Tend to the fields burning

The loser must be a king, I be
Holding queens (in captivity)
Queens to lay in beckoning
For a ruler, the jack of all trades

Short 1

You can go anywhere
Hang yourself there
You always have
More than enough
ROPE

Short 2

All that is created
Must come to a center
Twirling in subjective unity
About a common axis

Short 3

I am Man!
Give me time to create
I shall destroy much

Short 4

These days are the simple things
Close and closer
I find them fascinating
The more I try, the less they move

Short 5

I feel her breath move against my chest
Settling my darting thoughts
Her love lies in the mundane
In the common act

Down

The light is slowing down
Becoming long and burdened
Dragging though the trees and
Scraping across the mountain peaks

The air has followed suit
Sitting still upon the grass
Waiting for the chill to dry it out
As it gazes to the sky

Clouds have settled in and
They have found the light
Brilliant, reflective and now
It is their turn to shine

Washing up the day
Sitting down in the still
Feeling close but quiet
We hold hands a little longer

Without task-tinted eyes
We can now see each other
We are open in this moment
Still, beautiful, breathing

Kind

Pulling of Three

A blessed anger ran away with the cook
Managing to blanket the underground
In an increasingly dark embrace
Pulling up the flowered roots
Now ready to bloom yet again
Sending migraine waves
Through the delicately bonded trio

One on the run from the humiliation
Time has spent itself on perfection
Now standing silent in the mess of noise
Contempt for the poison rises up
And anger now runs with him

The circus moves to another town
Another act jumps on fallen opportunity
The back bone finds alternative fulfillment
The one realizes his genius
The cook fixes breakfast

I Don't See It That Way

My mind has taken to stumbling
Schedules, dates and names
Faces, conversations and facts
Those are the memories of others
I only have space for the current
As if a spirit guides my eyes
The burning catches my thoughts

Don't judge me for caring less
Society sees the overwhelming
The importance of the irrelevant
And the mundane of the irresistible
I have come to ignore the point
To ignore all the points
I have tried, I really have
But can't hum along to your melodic tune
And I can't see all those adjustable opinions,
From a skinny mind
And a bird's-eye view

New and Improved

They pulled up the bucket
Dry, it reached the light
Atop the old well
It had been built of the finest
concepts and materials
Of a day-long past
Built to endure with good intent
Built to endure the test of time
But the bucket had been drug and bounced
Up the roughly structured walls
Although tired and used;
The bucket tried with all its grain and might
To hold and deliver the life-sustaining fluid
From the deep of the well

Still it came up empty

So they all stared
Disappointment
Filled the air
Some walked away in disgust
Other sent the bucket down in a situational attempt at insanity
Then a few stood about the bucket
Deep in analysis, conversation and collusion
Agreeing that a new bucket was in great need
They argued, proposed, debated and settled;

It would be fashioned of the finest:
Concepts and materials of the modern day
Soon it would provide all
Provide all with all they need
Bigger, better, faster…
A greater idea of things indeed.

Middle

We can break the rust
Turn that bolt
Loosen the grip
But the saints
—The dealers
—The angels
—The demons
They can never bring us down

We are the true grit
Between the 1% and the bottom
We know the machine
—Its churning
—Its yearning
—Its hunger
Without us it would emaciate
It would stall
Decay
Wither
No one else can fix it
Add on to it
Or make it purr

Not you who is entitled
You can't do without us
Damn those that meddle with it
You will never keep us to the side
We will go where we please
Because we are the middle of it all

Sunflowers

The days of the roses are gone
Let the sunflower shine
Tracking the arching light
And then bowing to the stars

Respect is on the rise
Reaching for the heavens
Spreading roots to the core
Outgrowing this fertile plain

The steel is sitting quiet
Soaking up the rust
It dares not budge
Lest it be buried alive

The tangle of our minds
Will not hold us back
The uncertainty of our hesitation
Will not leave us to wonder

We have waited long enough
Crouching among the pines
Time to spread to the fields
Breathing in the flowering breeze

Forgetting

The city waits for no one,
Not to listen and learn.
Waiting for time to stall
Leave them hanging a constant
They come and fall into this unfamiliar landscape
Here they come to forget
Submerging themselves in the beauty
That runs thin across these intrepid earth tones
They are quick to unleash their influence
Then slam the door behind them
For too many have now trampled
Over their freshly made tracks in the snow
Here the outside is cherished
Then kept to the outside
"The problem is" is heard upon the air
Just as much as the air upon the trees
One's validity is not acquired upon factual regard
Rather it is determined upon time endured
Thus it is the ultimate measure of stature

I Forgot

When a date is made under comparable time constraints
Is it misinterpretation of the details?
Or does the forgetful mind believe only in tentative engagements?
Irritation is converted to disenchantment
There will be no date today
And there will be no excuses given
For the forgetful see no reason to explain their shortcomings
There is no observance of the other
Diagnoses cannot reflect upon one's self
Self is the only truth we have
And self in the end is not always one's fault
The forgetful must simply be forgotten

Throw Them Back

Unproductive transient
Grimy and unkempt
They gather in rope-headed individuality
They live in a throwback,
Someone else's sentimentality
Back to an ideology thrown away
And a generation failed
No new footsteps are being taken
Decades wasted following
Following the axe slinger
From one venue to the next
Futile attempts to recapture,
But time and time again it all fell short
Carry the recorded memory
Cherish it one above another
Just maybe they will induce some originality
But now the truckin' lifestyle is gone
Scattering them all about to deal
With the reality of the now

The King

If I could sit on a throne
Balanced atop a peak
Throw about orders
Stomp on the weak

I would drive the biggest
The reddest Cadillac there be
Riding about my domain
For all my servants to see

Drowning in jealousy
Other kings would scream
I'd show them just
How trivial it must seem

To be ruler of nothing
A king of dirt
Caked under my nails
The truth sure do hurt

But it's still my dirt
Running amuck about the page
Bringing down another star
To deal with a simpleton's rage

Unleashed

When time can't buy its own way
And the politicians run out of slogans
Society will come to a rest uneasy
The caretakers will wander aimlessly away
From this moment will come the torrent
Of a community's forgotten wishes
We will drive forward with our horns
Lancing the ruthless beast of civilization

Sure to Last

Dreams rest high and dry
Up on the lonesome road
People here wonder too long
Just wondering where to go

Can't tell where they're from
Don't want to know their past
They're looking for a sign
Something strong and sure to last

For those that live among this creed
They're watching to the west
For a new day that won't start
Among the savior and his guest

For love of him and love of me
They work the fields of stone
Don't worry for the broken hearts
'Cause they're all comin' home

Misguided she ran from me
Head-long out into the storm
But the sun has captured her
And healed her soul, tumbled and torn

So I lit out for the hills
Straight from being born
The words will leak out of me
They're all wicked, tired and worn

Something strong and sure to last
Something strong and sure to last
Somewhere on earth, there is something
Strong and sure to last

Weight

His varsity jacket
Hangs
Three sizes too big
Weighing her shoulders
Like the promise
She made

Back Again

Won't you break me down
My friend
Won't you take me back
My friend
This wheel has rolled around
Again
Over and over
Round and round
And back again
My friend

Inside

Checking In

Sometimes I have to check in with myself
Remind myself of what I can't see
Hidden behind the pillars of noise
That rise up from the valley floor
The opportunity on the wings of finches
Opening up tiny doors of righteousness
May these reminders always lead me
Take my hand and guide me
To a beautiful burden of love
A love of timeless wanting
Pulling and pushing the fear from me
Posting up the anger and cutting it down
There is one reminder that never comes to soon
Never comes behind the realizations
It's that sweetness does exist
There is a space where my heart lives free
Somewhere between that one and the next
Open to the wind under a bluebird sky
And within the confines of my self-discovery

Chasing

I am not sure what my mind is chasing about,
But a curious ghost has lured me into the woods
I fear you can no longer track me down
And I can no longer find my way back
For the last days snow has covered my steps

As I stand here listening to the silence
In this grove of trees there are no stumps
Nor rocks or fallen logs
No place to rest and ponder
In comfortable thought
There is just the silence
Covered in soft winter sounds
Snow falls from the branches
Down to the blanketed ground
Creek water wandering around rocks
Sealed beneath the growing ice
A bird I do not know calls out
To a silent hidden partner

As I stand, the cold slowly works its way in
Chilling me to discomfort
It reminds me of past decisions made
My discomfort grows like the disruptive air
Bellowing from the valley
Building like a rush of adrenalin from my belly,
The wind, uncaring and swift
It jumps at me from all around
Swiping at my feet
And sends the silence scurrying
Driving the cold always inwards

But for all its might
I keep my feet strong to the snow
The heat from my soul
Beats back the sting of the cold
In short, the wind abandons me
Moving along up and over the ridge
Down to the valley beyond and on again
The silence crept out from the pine boughs
And the cliff side crevices

I was left to chase my mind
Through the aspens and pines
As it has left the silence behind
And now is finding its way home

Hiding Things

I can ambush myself on occasion
It comes at me via undisciplined ways
Granted, it comes less upon less
Like the thought of my best friend
That has been some time now
But this other is short in time
So I flirt with shiny distractions
And fill my mind through risky ventures
Hidden but not discarded
I tuck away the notes and such
Trip lines with subtle advances
Await my every move
For hiding places are like dogs
Faithful and predictable

Judgement

I have used this body
Beyond its capabilities
Throwing it against adversity
Against life itself
Like tomorrow was a deception
Or someone else's problem
Life was just another object
Set up to be beaten
Beaten with this flesh
Beaten with this muscle
Beaten with persistence
Now the scar tissue is full
Laced up and stiff
I now sit in reflection
For sitting is better
I now throw experience
Throw it straight at me
I now let pain guide me
As daily reminders
Where it was to be overcome
Now it is to be respected
I have few choices
My bad judgement
Has taught me well
But every now and again…

Hero

Young, I first subscribed to forgetting
As I dwelled there among the masses
Preaching ideals of social corrosion
Armed with implements of greed
The intoxicating voices chanted
The haves…the have nots

Being naïve, I sought out simplicity
In accommodation I chose to forget
Entrenching myself in this exceeding Paradise
I was altogether solvent
But all around me churning expansion waged on
Here I stood indifferent yet knowing less
After all, this gave me less to forget

Tales from the masses returned
And before the eye has had a chance to confirm,
The rumors are all played out.
Myths and aspersions converted
Into plausible facts on mentally fabricated scenes

This land holds no words
Even with all that is said
Even with all that we drag though the brush
Fragmented statements contorted
Interpretation by personal bias
Dispatched from one ear to the next
I have now created the tragic, delinquent hero
They so love to tear down.

Communication

Don't ever steal from me my sanity
Or deny of me personal interaction among the masses
I don't want to be herded into crowded obscurity
Or play your territorial pissing games
This would stab me in the back despite my human dignity

I have no desire to be everywhere at once
A digital being hurled about the world
No face or body to gesture with
Leave me to converse with the person:
With body language, attitudes and reactions

Please, I beg of you, go run with the bulls!
Leave me to wander about the mountain flowers
Leave me to story about in great detail
With the reality of a person before me
This is what must be called existence

Motivation

I'm not very motivated this morning
A spark has left my side
Through the bed
Across the floor
To the wall
And out the door

Jumping up into the cab
Of the wandering wind

It broke off into pieces
With my mind's eye in tow
Watching in step
Watching it go

So here I really lie
Not very motivated this morning

Sleep Walking

We all set to walking
With sleep in our eyes
Lending to wicked dreams
Bowline to the bowel
A plague to the mind
Images of the turmoil
Offered up by daily events
HOLD ME DOWN!
Don't let me wander
Among the sleepless
To negotiate my thoughts
Compromise the immediate
For it can't be important
Qualifiers stand to reason
With you and your esteem
Pulling me down to the down
Defusing my nerves
Arrival REM three

In My Head

I wish the phone would stop ringing
I just want to lie here in seclusion
To rest and to forget
Watch these waves reach out from the ocean
Grabbing at the land as if they wanted to jump up,
Sit down beside me and enjoy a cold beer
There it goes again, reaching out to me
Laying its wanting across the wanting sands
Help me…save me…give me sanity
But I just want to sit
Sit and stare with dust-covered eyes
Stare so hard I can almost feel the ocean's pain
The sand is all spread out and irritated
It wishes the ocean would wash it all away
Tumble it about as if in a big washing machine
Then neatly place it back
To dry out where it had begun
Glistening with pride and renewal
Yeah, that's what the sand wishes
It also wishes that damn phone would stop ringin'

Infinity

Ten mighty giants displayed
My feelings brightly
Upon a canvas
Breaking up the contrast
Of the landscape so brilliant

Sticks and stones
Of peculiar nature and luster
Sit in waiting
Drawing you into my insanity
Send you to break up
My perfect day

Too many times the hammer
Has become myself
Drowning out the delicate
Balance this union should hold
But the nails must be driven

Eastern Rain

I'm your perfect little creature
Dwelling in your perfectly simple world

Running from deception
Desperately seeking that space
Railed with rusty iron hooks
A place to hang my soul

I run like a hot knife
Cauterizing an open wound
Then dance like a bull
Through china shop clichés

I have felt the sun's rays
Blister this sinner's face
Issuing lies at every crossroads
I'm one step ahead of dusk

I sympathize with the weak
And trample upon the poor
I'm not a savior of hearts
Nor a crusader of the masses
But a warrior of the indifferent
Trapped in the battle between
Faith and the way of the right
Knowing
No one can I level to

Standing dead and limbless
A needle among the green
Wildflowers flourish about me
But for one shaking moment

I will choose the deeper path
An emotional alignment
A blissful state, all ending up to matter
A containment of brute substance
Leaving behind a legacy,
Not hindered by time
I will find acceptance in feelings
Certain I shall never possess

With functional delusions
My sun falls from the sky
My moon refuses to show
Its soothing, silky face

The rain now drizzles a constant
From the East, cold on my barren skin
Fall is settling in
Now ending my summer of risk

What I See

Simplicity you see
Complication you be
Slowing you down
Running you around

That bird must fly
Oh why can't I
Up to the crisp
Diving to risk

You can hear
I can steer
Take us anywhere

Thin

My mind is dragging its feet
Like a child to an unwanted bedtime
I find distraction in the cobwebs
In the corner of the room
Where my ideas get lost
And the light runs thin

Influence

Well, I remember what you said and
I know what I did
But I can't remember anything in between
And nobody cares and they won't fill me in
And there are some things I just can't believe
Like how she talked about me that way
The way she talked about you the other day
I just can't understand
Her influence on me

Everything

Stomping
That is it
All about
Here to there
Even on
The in-between
Over water
Over ice
Over dirt
And stone
Stomping
The brush
Is tall
Knee-high
Brittle
It sounds clean
Beneath my feet
Maybe
I should
Drive

Head-Long

How much more can you open,
What is already open?
When you look at me,
Is there empty space?
Is it full of nothing but,
Humility and grace?

If you're able take a look through me
This will be where the real story starts
On the miles of cobblestone lanes
Winding in self-preservation and pride
Rolling over the hills of regret
Yet despite this long way around
I have not made it to the present yet

Lyrical

Broken Love Songs

The mountains turned into someplace,
I'd already been
The sun, it set gently upon my heart
And I couldn't say when it was I fell apart
Something tells me it's all wrong
And the radio's only playing broken love songs

For three days, she shared her love with me
For three days, it was love beyond belief
Can't shake this feelin' of loneliness
Can't shake this feelin' of being blessed
I'm finding it hard to stand up straight and strong
And the radio's only playin' broken love songs

She stared straight through me with those eyes of blue
She stared straight through me with a love so true
The taste of her lips, they're oh so sweet
The feel of her body, knocks me off my feet
Now I can't believe my baby, she done gone
And the radio's only playin' broken love songs

Fly On

You might be a rusted angel
But somehow you always sparkle for me
A guiding light through the timbers
I'm lost without you, can't you see?

I will look to the west for your silhouette
I will listen for you on this ocean breeze
My crazy heart will always wonder
Baby, why did you set me free?

You were created a woman
An everloving passionate soul
I loved you for all the right reasons
Baby, why did you have to go?

Fly on, fly on rusted angel
Free yourself to the wind and the rain
Free yourself from the ties that bind
Free yourself from all of your pain

Fly on, fly on rusted angel
Free yourself to the wind and the rain
Just remember there's a simple man
And an open heart that still remains

Stunning

She's the rhythm of the ocean
And the breeze through the trees
She's my little baby
Show some respect if you please

She's got a voice like an angel
She can rock down the house
She's my little baby
Beyond a shadow of a doubt

She's so sweet on me
Always treats me right
She's my little baby
Ain't no fussing, ain't no fight

She holds my heart
Never leaves me blue
She's my little baby
She's so kind and she's so true

She's stunning
No other way to say it
Look my way
Call my name
I can barely take it

Otherwise

I'm asleep at the wheel
You can't tell me otherwise
I broke your heart and messed up your mind
You can't tell me otherwise

My momma's words they don't ring true
I was never a good son to her
And I was never good to you
And you can't tell me otherwise

People telling me what to do
But they don't have the clues
And they don't know what I did to you
And you can't tell me otherwise

We'll move on and forget all the pain
We'll fall in love
But it will never be the same
And you can't tell me otherwise

When I Cry

Keep it all
Keep it right
Keep me wrapped up tight

Run the race
Run me around
Run me into the ground

Roll me low
Roll me high
Roll me away when I cry

Show me how
Show me wrong
Show me all night long

Worry for me
Worry for the sky
Worry for me
And don't ask why

Cruelty

The nightly hours
Cold howlin' wind
People run for cover
Runnin' from their sins

She looks at him
Young, confused together
Takes his place behind the wheel
Around the corner, gone forever

Traces on the mirror
Razor blade in hand
Cutting off reality
Come on, join the band

Fork in the road
Which path to choose
Maybe the one most traveled
Maybe either way, you lose

All grown up
Your path is chosen
Life is in your hands
But your hands are frozen

Psychs analyze it
Mothers say beware
But it's just life
For some a nightmare

Spinning

The sun went down
And the sky turned red
That's about the time that
I got out of bed

I hit the ground a runnin'
And I ain't lookin' back
Headin' down this highway
On a one-way track

I'm on a one-way track
Headin' down the line
One more drink, one more bar
And a hell of a time

My mind is spinning
Gin and tonic kickin' in
My mind is spinning
Bartender set me up again

Getting lost in the whiskey
Barstool suckin' me in
Can't look in the mirror
Livin' in this life of sin

Wakin' up rusted
Down on the desert floor
I'll never ask for much
But I will always ask for more

Yeah, You can roll me baby
All night long
You did nothing wrong
You did
You did nothing wrong

Baby Come

Baby dance and baby roll
Baby come and rock my soul
Baby want and baby scream
Baby come and rescue me

Rescue me
Come and
Rescue
Me

Heart

Moving On

Throwing stones
Breaking bones
Swinging sticks
Bleeding lips

Labels worn
Public scorn
Raised fist
Apologetic kiss

She talked her way
    Into it
She's swinging her way
    Out of it

Mending thought
Movement taught
Personal wealth
Loving self

Brilliance

You're a shining light
Positive, warm and bright
Don't sacrifice your brilliance
Not just for circumstance
Make your voice true and clear
Project it out devoid of fear
Stand with your heart forward
And your sights upward
Stay the course you see fit
And let your inner self emit

Burn

I will not whimper and whine
Nor stumble out into this life
But I will stand before the ends
Raging far beyond my burn
Outward and up, past the stars
I will rage about my emotions
My innermost desires
Running them through opposition
Up against the will of the impossibility
I will rage into this life

Sheep

The political drone
You must fight against
Make up your mind
And speak your sense
Don't do what they ask
Don't take sides so blind
Defend your thoughts
And leave the pack behind

'Til Next Time

I have no expectation
No preconception
But if we are to meet
Maybe again some day
Please make sure it is free
From any and all deception

Daughter

If she asks
I will say…

Be present
Where you are.
Be aware
Of your happiness.
Be loving
toward whom you're with
Take time
To find your bliss

These things don't
Come easy
Nor quick in time
But search
And you will find
They can fulfill
Your body
Soul and mind

Trust

Fall into me
    I will catch you
Walk away from me
    I will let you go
Stand up to me
    I will understand you
Go along with me
    I will shun you
Live for your happiness
    I will walk beside you
Put yourself in my hands
    I will drop you
Live to be you
    I will believe in you
Sleep beside me
    I will comfort you
Worry for the weak
    I will support your cause
Want not of me
    I will set you free
Stand behind me
    I will fall into you

Bring Us In

I've been round and round
And over this again
You're a beautiful woman
And an old soul friend

You'll hold me up
And bring me in
Treat me sweet
Without deception

What I see
And what you know
No place to hide
No place to go

I try to understand
Maybe I never will
How you look so good
How you fill my fill

Now the past was a test
Just to see what we will do
Stand up and fight
Or give up what we grew

Life has taken hold
To drag us here
Filled us with hope
Dashed all our fears

Now wash away the past
Never break this gaze
Hold each other true
Each other we shall raise

Others

Sleep Deep

Sleep with beauty in the mind
With perfection on the tongue
Sleep with ospreys on perch
And with buffalos on the run
The world will be tranquil for your thoughts
The universe at ease
So take in the goodness
And take the night to breathe
Do this all
So as to let tomorrow shine

Heads Up

There is love out there
But there is a lot of hate
If you choose to recognize the hate
    (well, then…)
The hate will recognize you
Now I'm not saying,
The whole world is crazy,
Wild at heart
    …and evil
But keep your head up
and protect that innocent smile
While you evaluate
Investigate
and figure out just what you support

Live the life you desire
With respect to others
Never compromising your
    Integrity
Go right ahead and take all you want
Yet eat all you take.

Should I Think?

She asked,
What are you thinking right now?

Ambiguous but to the point

But with all due respect to the events
Which have just played themselves out
Upon this laden bed

What am I thinking?

Is there something else?
That could possibly penetrate
My deviant mind?
A woman's lust has just been laid upon me
With irrefutable power

Disabling my cognitive skills
And setting me all about
I have no thoughts beside my gratitude
I won't take the easy way out

Starry Nights

Closing the eyes
From endless stars
The shadows emerge
Drawn from the darkness
And laid transparent
Across a lusting plain
Taken up before me
An adventure, to explore
A deepening abyss
Quickening my sense
I hunt for pleasures
Horizons surround me

Desperately searching
About the darkness
Voices hinting of
Facial expressions
Bodily movements expressing
Intents behind the mood

Somewhere before me
In all the ether
Lies the perfect spot
That single place
Set aside in time
The place which overwhelms the stars
Sending them to expand
With uncontained bliss

The spot in the rhythms
Bring us together, locked

Disconnected
Yet acutely aware
Of all within us
Surging up from an abyss
Thrown into brilliant light
Bathed with the uncontrolled
Joy from wonderment found

The shadows gently creep back in
The stars slowly
Steadily
Regain
Consciousness

Tranquil Waters

Dancing and singin'
    I missed the rain
Shuckin' and jivin'
      Right through the pain

Tranquil waters
Trusting daughters
Endless skies
Bloodshot eyes

Swingin' you around
    I peeled back the rind
Kissin' and smoochin'
    I was short on time

Family photos
Quiet mottos
Dusty trails
Memory fails

Sittin' and wishin'
    Quiet burning reflection
She's all gone
        All what's left is rejection

Details

You are not painted with broad strokes
Left about to fade into the panorama
Your ways lie in my simplicity of being simple
I find you in the slightest of motions
The tiniest of notions
Bursting forth in a multitude of droplet memories
You are settled in the subtleness of my day
Tagging on to my darting thoughts

Deep of You

You didn't know I was looking
But I caught that side of you
Caught it looking oh so sweet
I was not sure if it was the light
Or if you quietly let me in
For a second I saw inside you
I saw your heart beat
Beat with all the beauty
Of all of you
It was all like I had pictured you
And in that moment
You almost gave it away
Your deepest part of you
Please don't worry
It is all safe with me
I hold you in me only for me
You are what I hold

Care

"I care for her," he said
Mostly to himself but out loud
Not knowing from what
Not knowing from where
Nor could he see why he cared
But saying it made him thick
In the throat and the head
There was nothing solid to hold
Just an authentic truth could stick
Down beneath his ribs
Where physical emotions hide
It was all he could be
On this introspective ride

Intrepid steps forward
Into an emotion
Care

I'm the Fool

"Fools rush in," they say
But who are they to make up
This chronological timeline of love
Now it's like, now it's good,
Now it's love, now it's right
Cast out your vows upon a congregation
    So neat and tidy, prim and proper
Does truth and respect hold more
Over time and duration?
Does the time make feeling viable?
Are they more content and at ease?
Wait another moment
    And this one is gone
This one is full of mixed emotions,
    Wonderment and life
This is my now and my thought
Not time in context to others
Let the context take care of itself
I will play the fool

Stay In Me

Slowly and in short time I wove her in
Deep into the fabric of my life
Fabric slightly tattered yet still soft and taut
Not a thread can be pulled without effect
Not without emotions running long through the weave
Kicking off a stream of memories
Undeniable kindness, appreciation and understanding

Now one year has passed to the next
She has chosen her way of trying to understand
Understanding who she is and what is next
This is not my place nor is there space

I have quickly grown heavy with dust
That heavy you get from a broken heart
Not broken from love that was lost
But broken from love that was had
One that I have no words for
For I have never had this before
Nor have I ever had anything so exquisite

I don't want the threads to fade
I don't want the connections to be undone
I have wrapped myself up in the silk,
The cotton and comforting wool.
I feel warm here

These memories around me
Her perfection will not soon fade
Attached to the fiber of me
I have nothing more but to stay

Gone the Day

Factory-produced doubt
Has the leaves on the run
Soon the wind will blow
Blow away the light
Sending it to the south
I will stand to see
See the love I missed
She will be gone
Gone to the woods
Lost to the mountainside
Swept down running streams
To the bottom of the cold, deep lakes
The winter's ice will shut her in

Love of Dogs

This pain has filled up my consciousness
Confused my reactions to decision
Once easily made
Stealing away my mind to dreams of pleasure
Pleasures that are just torturous memories

Here in this willing of all places
I have experienced something unique
An emotional bond between two souls
Now the bond is broken

To pick up and leave was once second nature
Now there is hesitation
In sluggish regret I collect up my life
My packages of burden moved
In lethargic disposition

I'm thinking of a love not yet finalized
Of experiences undone

Disinclined, I now move ahead
Toward some unknown destination
Like a dog on a long-running leash

On Me

Pour yourself on me
Drench me in your soul
Wrap me up in your warmth
Life has taken its toll

The universe challenged me
Your words set me straight
Society challenged me
Your support is that of fate

Pour yourself on me
Letting my mind feel free
To dance with your thoughts
To let it be what it will be

What could be so bad?
Is there somewhere else you need to be?
I just need to ask of you
Pour yourself on me

For You

World came along
Said you look like you need some help
Woman came along
Said you love no one but yourself

Heartache came along
Told me you better run and hide
Woman came along
Said lift yourself up, bury your pride

Society came along
Said stay down and don't speak up
Woman came along
Said listen to others, fill up your cup

Now I am just livin' for you
Just livin', dancin' and singin'
For you.

All Lit-up

I will force you back in the shadows
Always there, but hard to see
Small crumbs of your tender love
A trail leading you back to the light
But I can only let you briefly stay
A short distraction from the present
If you stay too long, I will slow
And the light will stumble and wane
So take your piece back to the back
A warm place tucked away in my mind
A place soft and comfortable to touch
Please do not dislike me for this tactic
For I must protect me
From when you're all lit-up
There, shiny feelings are laced
With delayed dull pain
Visitation limits must be implemented
This is good for my heart
You back in the back
I will see you soon, I promise

1% to All

I seem to have misplaced a part of me
Or should I say a part has chosen to leave
Despite the overwhelming attachment
And the mutual agreement of connection

So take a good look at me
Just how much do you see?
Is the missing part evident to you?
Or is it something that I can only feel?

I am for sure at least 1% short
Just 1%
Unfortunately, as it so happens,
That 1% made up a deep part of me

That not-so-small piece was woven in
Woven tightly into the fabric of my life
Not a thread can be pulled
Not one that doesn't stimulate a memory
Leading to another stitch, a connection
Another memory in turn comes alive

The absence of 1% has altered me
Letting me believe in all I thought impossible
Although I am short all so much
I have grown and gained tenfold

Too Quick

I could fall back into you
    Too quick
You know this
That is why you stand
    Too close
You feel this

I wish you around me
    Too much
You don't mind
That is why you talk
    Too soft
You understand

Slip Away

Just now it happened
I felt you slip away
Out through my finger tips
Down into the water
Under the water
Under the stone
Down into the mud
Still yourself
Don't stir a twitch
Slip away
Softly
Slip away

Every Day

You told me once,
"You have texted me good morning,
Every day, since we have met."
I thought about this
It was not premeditated
Not part of some plan
Or ever thought of as such
It was just what I did

I have realized
I have said good morning to you
Every day, since you left
Sometimes out loud
Sometimes in my head
This has not been premeditated
Not part of some plan
Or ever thought of as such
It is just what I do

Morning After

I'm back and forth
Upside down
In and out
And all around

I'm running and doing
Here and there
Up and down
All together nowhere

And here she lies
Without laying
The scent of essential oils
Sweat, fingertip memories
Her voice echoes from the paint
Bringing me to a center
She was here
That did happen

I'm now taking a minute to remember

Underneath It All

There is something to be said about nothing
And nothing to be said about what you done
Wishful thinking and mindful notions
This will wish away a few wasteful days
But you can't pretend like it didn't happen
Like the story never was fully told
These chapters of your wicked ways
Read as if they have a dance in words
A sweet, succulent, seductive dance
Forcing the stares of intrigue and judgement
You draw in the innocent bystander
These stories will hang in the balance
While you wash away the fingerprints
Left by your greasy fingers of drama

Black Water

The way it all went down
Left me thinking real hard
Like being alone
Might be the best thing by far
Maybe I'm good for no one
Maybe it's just you
But I have to face the faces
And babe so do you

So I'll pack my things
And a couple things more
You won't have to deal with it
Never again, that's for sure
Don't look through the window
That would be too damn mean
Your back door man will be along
Oh so fresh and clean

So out and about and down the road I go

Black water risin'
I'm caught in its wake
Black water risin'
Make no mistake
I am down the road
My soul you did break.

Four Winds

The four winds converged
Blowing a pure
Unyielding
Chill
She stood alone
Precariously on the steep edge
Here the wind swayed her
Above the rocky valley
To and fro
My blood pounding
My veins constricting
Anticipation ran deep
I could use a little direction
A guide to my confusion
Maybe just a bit of happiness
Just a little for now

Will she fall?

Blurry

Blurry I wake this morning
Lying still as nausea heats my face
The sun light pierces my eyes
I pray you have not remembered all of last night
The reverend was preaching up such a captivating sermon
Drenching me in that brown water baptism
Violently raising the spirits up within me
Stirring up suppressed feelings of indignity
Subconscious truths slurred from my wicked tongue
Departing from the norm my tirade came unannounced
Soaking you in bitterness
Like a storm's first downpour
No shelter could you reach
The thunder beating at your innocent ear
Running you off before the lightning could strike

So I sat, a blustery king on my three-footed throne,
Alone I sat to rule my domain
Intoxicated court jesters danced about me
Justifying my claim and toasting my rule

But now I lay in my suffocating sheets
Awaiting your call—or should I reach out?
So we can meet once again
On that battlefield of words
Where you can make a great offensive
Me trying to stitch it all back together
Words forming accusations, assumption,
And possibly sweet nothings

Out of nothing but regret comes
Empty apologies
They come from me in smooth tones of fear
We will meet on some shaky, common ground
Yet tomorrow I will inevitably wake with another headache

Dedication

Stories You Told

We gathered in our corner of the world
Where the trees overtake old farms
The water is restrained below our watch
Where the house is familiar and telling
The creaky boards bringing long memories
Where the fire warms the family
The place where you sang your stories of life

You told of flights of adventure
Of the girl you made your one and only
You told of children's play and misadventure
Of scouts and adolescent football heroes
You told of mountains and snow to play upon
Of sleeping with the bears on summer nights
You told of nature and cooking with fire
Of soil tilled for the growth of beauty
You told of number puzzles on market walls
Of service to others and higher powers
You told of stones, formations and ancient seams
Of trilobites caught in the sediments of time
You told of virtues to guide our lives
Of friends and neighbors to share our table
You told of love until you fell asleep

Here in our corner of the world
Beside the open hearth
You told stories
Stories I never thought I would miss

To Old Father Laemmel

www.ingramcontent.com/pod-product-compliance
Lightning Source LLC
Chambersburg PA
CBHW032044290426
44110CB00012B/947